ENJOY THE DANCE

SIMON HAINES

2023

Published by Rosewood Press

Hadleigh Suffolk

© Simon Haines 2023

www.rosewoodpress.co.uk

Author's other works
- It's Nuts
- Sea Planes and Seed Trays
- For the meek
- Quietly quaking
- This is not a baguette

ISBN 978-1-7398759-6-1

CONTENTS

Enjoy the dance	1
A photo of my mother	2
Cheers Dylan	4
Night-time dash	5
Hope of change	7
Human limitations	8
Larkin letters	9
Snow aglow	10
Elvis night	11
Muntjaccident	12
Amusing my dad	14
Sea planes	15
One evening in May	16
Meeting an old friend	17
My daily walk	18
Things that are pointless	19
Slight defect	20
Nine across "Memory loss"	21
Five o'clock in the morning	22
Gallery souvenirs	23
Egret in the river	25
Go down your own end	26
Shower time	27
A crack of light	28
My spare recorder	29
Heath	30
Our empty high street	31

About the author	32
About Rosewood Press	34

ENJOY THE DANCE

Lying
Squirming
Crawling
Toddling
Walking Walking
Dancing Dancing Dancing Dancing
Walking Walking
Swaying
Staggering
Falling
Lying

A PHOTO OF MY MOTHER – A SESTINA

That's my mum you're dusting
On the wall of our spare room
She was only three years old.
An unfocused black and white photo,
Taken on a warm spring day,
Long before she was my mother.

She wouldn't have dreamt of being a mother
Or that one day she'd love dusting
Doing it several hours a day
Singing from room to room
Cleaning every bauble and photo
And thinking she'd never grow old.

She married at twenty-one years old
To the delight of her father and mother
Sweet smiling in her white wedding photo.
The maids had been hard at work dusting
In that post-war bridal bedroom
Where my parents spent all the next day.

Seven years later on a bright May day
At twenty-eight years old
She gave birth to me in an upstairs room
And so became my mother.
That day there'd been no dusting
And nobody took a photo.

The world first saw me in a small photo
In my cot on a winter's day.
Mum spent all her time dusting
I'd have been six months old,
But despite being busy, my mother
Kept checking on me in my room.

Sixty years later in a different room
Graced by one family photo
I went to a care home to see my mother
She had no idea of the time or the day,
And, feeling neither young nor old,
Had forgotten all about dusting.

Today, I too am feeling old.
I won't be dusting anything in any room,
Except for that monochrome photo of my mother.

CHEERS DYLAN!

It is spring, moonless night in the small town,
Starless and bible-black.

It was such a night last Tuesday
as we emerged from A & E.
With your ankle tightly bandaged,
you'd slipped on the morning's icy path.
I was ready to drive us home.

The hospital car park was still like glass
when we reached our aged Skoda.
Its iced-over windows were sparkling white.
But sadly, we'd forgotten to bring
our scraper or de-icing spray.

We got in the car, turned on the heat
and waited for the ice to melt.
You said: "We could use that
CD case in the glove box
To scrape the ice off the window."
It was the one we'd bought last summer
and have listened to several times since:
Richard Burton reading Under Milk Wood.
Of course it worked a treat.

Cheers Dylan!

NIGHT-TIME DASH
After Goethe's *Erköning*

Who's that driving so furiously
on this stormy, windy night?
It's a father with his sickly son,
keeping him warm, holding him tight.

Father grips the wheel with steely dread.
No help had arrived that night.
He's risking his life and the life of his son
and consumed by mortal fright.

Through nervous delirium and half-closed eyes,
ghostly spirits the sick boy sees.
"It's just silvery mist," the father swears
"swirling in the breeze."

"Those spirits have asked me to come with them,"
protests the unquiet child.
Once more the father calms the boy:
"It's the wind that's blowing wild."

"No! No!" objects the sickly boy,
now ecstatic and clear in his mind
"I have to go! I need to go!
Father, please be kind!"

Holding his child tighter,
father drives on but,
arriving at the doors of A and E,
he knows his son has gone.

HOPE OF CHANGE

Transformation in ways of thinking,
sinking in acres of battlefield mud -
blood where tanks, smoke belching
squelching selfless defenders to death
breath extinguished in ill-fitting boots
grassroots offer no firm foothold.

It's an ordinary dreary day as we snoop,
troop sadly round our shelled-out town,
down through cratered squares and streets
defeats mount up with citizens weeping
creeping silently from torture and rape
escape is not an option.

The morning may well bring us change –
rearrange this violent outcome
some will discover ways of touching
clutching hope and silently scrambling
gambling on some resolution
revolution, peace or prostitution.

HUMAN LIMITATIONS

Weeks below zero the hardest frost
has stopped all road and building work.
The frozen ground's too hard to dig
so labourers have moved to indoor work.

As we passed the now quiet building site,
I almost tripped and fell flat on my face
over the crumbly soft brown earth
of a recently thrown up mole hill.

LARKIN LETTERS

I read in this morning's paper
they've found more Larkin letters,
in one of which he bemoans the fact
that he's fat and going deaf.

They reckon these letters will probably fetch
thousands of pounds at auction.
So I thought maybe I'd write some myself;
you see I'm fat and going deaf, too.

SNOW AGLOW

finding snow aglow on the ground
grass like glass in morning frost
no sun yet to get us warmer
sleeping rough is tough enough
under bridges cold as fridges
in threadbare clothes those charities give us

humans lost or double-crossed
by lopsided or misguided structures
aiding not the poor or needy
but admitting the few who queue in line
to pass the test and line their nest
satisfying their greed but not our need

we'd like to think a chink in their shield
might bring about their final fall - all
tumbling while mumbling their innocence
neither innocent nor decent but guilty as charged
clutching their wealth by stealth acquired
they've always screwed you and spewed you out

ELVIS NIGHT

It was New Year's Eve in the care home
We were all dressed up to the nines.
Then we heard the terrible news
Elvis'd broken down near Lincoln,
With no chance of recovery that night.
We tried Buddy Holly but he was tied up
Doing a New Year's Eve gig in Burnley.
We were about to give up when someone said:
"Roy Orbison – have we still got his number?"
We searched high and low and telephoned Roy
We'd had him three years earlier.
He said he'd more than happy to come
It took him just an hour on the bus.
Ten minutes later in authentic gear
He emerged in the residents' lounge.
He started his set by singing "In Dreams"
Followed quickly by "Oh, Pretty Woman"
(Complete with the throaty growl.)
What had looked like being a disaster
Turned out a great success.
Roy Orbison had saved the day, but
Next year we'll try for Elvis again.

MUNTJACCIDENT

Most nights a muntjac visits us
and feeds peacefully on our plants.
Until today it's raced away
when we open the door at dawn
so fast you could barely see it,
out through our garden gate.

Today it simply stared at us
then sauntered casually away
untroubled by our being there.

Its favourite food is hydrangea
and latterly camelia leaves.
We wish it wouldn't eat our plants
so we shut the gate to keep it out.

One morning we found it munching
the last of our camelia leaves.
I opened the door and it tried to escape
but the garden gate was shut.

It panicked and rushed around
then climbed our garden wall,
then caught sight of itself
in a window, and, frightened, crashed right through
leaving broken glass and splashes of blood
on our neighbour's window sill.

It continued to panic once inside,
breaking furniture, wreaking havoc
then crashed back through
the window glass
and off it ran probably wounded.

AMUSING MY DAD

My dad would smile,
no doubt about it,
to see me wearing
his expensive jerkin.

He gave it to me
as part of scheme
to simplify his life
before moving to a sheltered flat.

He also offered me his ties
and couldn't believe it
when I told him I never wore a tie.
"What never?" he asked.
"No never,"

SEA PLANES

My granddaughter said in a serious tone
As she painted a unicorn pink
For no actual reason that I could discern
We're learning about sea planes this week.

Sea planes? I queried sounding slightly surprised.
My! The curriculum has broadened out!
No! Not 'sea planes'! she shrieked with a grin on her face
Why would we learn about them?

I said 'seed trays' she screeched. *Sorry!* I replied.
Was the problem her lisp or my deafness?
I've got a seed tray growing herbs in my shed
No! Not 'seed trays' she exploded, unable to hide
Her contempt for her poor old deaf granddad.

Listen attentively, watch my lips closely
I'll say it again very slowly
At school last week we started to learn
About 'Steam trains! not Seed trays or Sea planes!

ONE EVENING IN MAY

It was an evening in May
at a village dance.
The accordion was playing
a gentle waltz.
A young man entered -
He was keen to dance
with a girl he had seen
through the window.
He approached her and said
"May I dance with you?"
"Yes, of course," she said,
and stood up shyly.
At the end of the waltz,
he bowed, she curtsied.
"You're pretty," he whispered.
She blushed and looked down.

She was English. He was French.
Post Brexit - May 2023.

MEETING AN OLD FRIEND

Sorry I didn't recognise you,
but it is nearly forty years.
I can see it now though:
that look in your eyes,
your playful little smile
and the squeak you make
every time you laugh.

*I recognised you immediately
You don't look any different.*

But I'm fatter and greyer
and look miserable most of the time!

*You always looked miserable
That's how I knew it was you.*

MY DAILY WALK

I'm going for my regular walk today
To see a bird that's not always there.
It's sometimes there and sometimes not
I won't know till I'm near the river.

On occasions I've seen it somewhere else,
further up the water course,
wading, feeding and looking forlorn.
It may be awaiting me there.

Maybe it thinks I'm Godot.
I'm not.

THINGS THAT ARE POINTLESS   1

Particularly pointless are fingerless gloves.
Broken pencils and unrequited loves
Squat church towers and children's knives
Doc Martens boots and other people's wives.
Diced carrots and most people's ears

THINGS THAT ARE POINTLESS   2

Flossing your teeth twice a day
Not to save your teeth
But to prevent the pain inflicted
By a grumpy hygenist
Whose aim in life is
To stop you taking up the costly time
Of the smiling dentist
Now specialising
In lucrative root canal.

Paying fifty pounds to watch a Beckett play
Sitting there for 60 minutes
To be forced to confront
Your own end game, your own mortalité
It has been pointed out to me
And fair enough – I do agree
That lists like these are pointless too
As is true of poetree.

SLIGHT DEFECT

The four down clue *(6-6)*
Was *Slight defect*
What were synonyms for *slight*?
Came up with *trivial, little,* and *minor*
It must be *little*, or so I thought.
Great that's at least a start.
I moved on next to *defect*
Could be *blemish, fault,* or *weakness*
But none had just six letters.
Back to the drawing board - Sod it.

A clue across gave me a V
For the second word's first letter.
Then an S for the third
Little visits seemed possible,
But highly unlikely.
Then an N for the last letter.
Vision would fit
But *little-vision* meant nothing
And certainly not with a hyphen.

So I threw down my pen in frustration
And awaited the solution next day.
Tunnel vision was the answer.
I shrieked and looked back at the clue.
Clean spectacled and peering closely
I read again - 'kin hell
4 Down - *Sight defect (6-6)*

NINE ACROSS "MEMORY LOSS"

Got any letters?
Begins and ends with A
Sorry – can't remember.
There's a name for that, isn't there?
Name for what?
You know – for when you can't remember
The word for loss of memory.

Oh yes - No, don't tell me
It's on the tip of my tongue.
I knew I'd get it in the end
It's anaemia

FIVE O'CLOCK IN THE MORNING

It was five o'clock in the morning
when a pounding headache woke me,
I got up for a pee, a paracetamol
and a soothing cup of tea.
In the kitchen I felt a hunger pang.
Downstairs it was barely light.
Max would miaow for food
if he heard me or saw me move,
so I didn't turn the light on,
just tiptoed across the floor,
blindly towards the fruit bowl
to see what I could find.

I crept victorious back upstairs
and snuggled back into bed.
proclaiming to anyone still awake
"I found a banana in the dark."

GALLERY SOUVENIRS

We have a Grayson Perry hanky
that you wouldn't wipe your nose on
a detail from a tapestry
in yellow, green and crimson.

And a David Hockney cushion
that you wouldn't sit your arse on
twenty-seven quid it cost
A Bigger Splash in cotton.

And a Giacometti T-shirt
with a sculpture that's been sprayed on
a tall and very spindly man
looks more like I've spilt food on.

A fridge magnet by Matisse
a cut-out: Blue Nude Two
a sixteenth of the actual size
makes it easier to view.

And a Wassily Kandinski tea mug
Swinging 1925
finest white bone china
keeping "modern" art alive.

We've got nothing by Picasso yet,
that's something I'd quite like
Pants with Three Musicians
or Don Quixote on a bike.

EGRET IN THE RIVER

Every day we walk to glimpse
the egret in our river.
Sometimes it's there and sometimes not
We're not sure till we get there.

That doesn't stop us walking
it gives us motivation
while we're striding out and talking
about wildlife conservation.

The egret never makes a sound
It's silent, white and free
It may take flight and wheel around
then land high in a tree.

It struts around on spindly legs.
We've never seen a mate.
Will it ever nest and lay its eggs?
Will chicks appear one day?

GO DOWN YOUR OWN END

As kids, we lived in a cul-de-sac
with a "green" at the end of the sac.
It was round and covered in lush green grass
and was perfect for playing games on.

Our enemies lived round this green playground
and objected to us and our games.
They came out of their houses like venomous snakes
and shouted "Go down your own end!"

Minnie and her sister our most ferocious foes
were backed up by plump Mrs Padgem.
These three emerged grumpily from their homes
to shout: "Bugger off down your own end!"

In response, we targeted their sad little homes
With apples and clods of earth
Sometimes they called the local police,
who told us off with a wink and a smile.

I've no idea what became of Mrs Padgem
or Minnie and her sister
but oddly now that I'm seventy-eight
no one tells me to go down my own end.

SHOWER TIME

When Tom text he'd pop
Round in half an hour,
I said "I'm just about to hop
In our brand new shiny shower."

I should of course have said "into"
Cos it's sad but we all know it's true.
You really shouldn't hop in a shower
When you're almost seventy-two.

A CRACK OF LIGHT

As a child, going to bed could be an ordeal
once Mum and Dad were downstairs.
They read me a story and kissed me goodnight
before tucking me snugly in.

Though I didn't actually fear the dark
once they'd gone, I used to feel anxious;
so to keep in touch with the wide-awake world
my door was left slightly ajar.

So a thin crack of light could still be seen,
and a mumble of voices heard.
This helped me to sleep feeling safe and secure
not condemned to the darkness of night.

MY SPARE RECORDER

Is that my spare recorder
over there by the microwave?
That's an odd location.
It's only made of bakelite -
definitely not wood.
I'm wondering "Would it melt
if we cooked it on full power?
Or would the microwave explode?"

But hey - it's an instrument I sometimes play
And it's only slightly flat.
So let's not experiment – yet.

HEATH

There's a pagan cache on Dunwich Heath
and heather as far as Minsmere,
then across to Sizewell B - soon C
- rollers stream from east to west
silently from this high cliff.

A bird stands motionless, staring ahead
from yellow broom. Could it see me?
I stare back and hear its song.
Will it always sing so sweetly
as its habitat is annexed?

For now all's smugly peaceful here
but how long for - we've no idea.
Will there still be heath and still be birds?
We strain to listen for the answers we fear.

OUR EMPTY HIGH STREET

Our High Street's oddly quiet tonight,
no vehicles parked or passing through.
The whole scene drowns in dying light
Is this the night before the coup?

In the distance we hear the drowsy drone
of a cruel slow-moving truck
then insistently clicking metronomes
of rapid gun fire – we're dumbstruck.

Should we wait to witness what unfolds?
Or creep back home like frightened mice?
Our houses are not robust strongholds
Invaders wouldn't need to think twice.

A cyclist pedals past, then to our surprise,
from a single shot he falls and dies.

ABOUT SIMON HAINES

When I was 7, I went in for a national poetry competition for school children and, to my amazement, won second prize. The competition was to write an extra verse to *Old Mother Hubbard*. I was too shy to go to London to collect the prize, and sadly I didn't keep that extra verse as proof of my early promise.

I have always written poems and songs though few have seen the light of day until recently. Covid lockdowns gave me more time to write and more subjects to write about. Several of my poems have been included on the Poetry Wivenhoe Lockdown collection website, and two of these were included in their printed collection *Tales Told By Birds*. I have also had several poems published in Suffolk Poetry Society's *Twelve River Ripples*. Five of my political poems have been published in *The Morning Star*.

Other poems have been broadcast on BBC Radio Essex.

In my spare time, I play music in three groups:

The Hosepipe Band, a group which plays for ceilidhs and also accompanies poetry readings by Martin Newell and Blake Morrison.

Bof!, a quartet which plays French and Breton music for dances and concerts.

Rosewood, an acoustic trio which plays folk music in folk clubs and festivals.

ABOUT ROSEWOOD PRESS

Rosewood Press is a small independent set-up which publishes collections of poems and songs by poets and musicians, some of whom you may not know. Our current list:

ADRIAN MAY
- *Full Fathom Folk* – a collection of songs and poems. A CD of 14 of the songs recorded by Adrian and Face Furniture, with The Extensions is included with the book.
- *Preacher! – The Vanity Games* – a verse commentary of Ecclesiastes

KATH TAIT
- *An Odd Number of Songs* – Twenty-three of Kath's most well-known songs. Lyrics are accompanied by Kath's own illustrations and guitar chords.

SIMON HAINES
- *This is not a Baguette* – "Thirty five poems about things made of wood around my house."
- *Quietly Quaking* – "Light, but not unserious poems about the everyday … witty, compassionate – and occasionally biting." Adrian May
- *For the Meek* – A collection fifty poems

- *Sea Planes and Seed Trays* – Humorous, serious, political and nonsense poems and songs about relationships and current news.
- *It's Nuts* – a first collection of attempts at humour.

All the above are available from:
www.rosewoodpress.co.uk

Poets or songwriters who would be interested in having collections published, should contact Simon Haines. We might be able to work something out.

Contact - 07818 417780 / simonhaines1@icloud.com

www.ingramcontent.com/pod-product-compliance
Lightning Source LLC
Chambersburg PA
CBHW040510110526
44587CB00044B/4158